15 MYTHS, MISTAKES, AND MISREPRESENTATIONS ABOUT THE DEUTEROCANON

By Gary Michuta

NIKARIA PRESS

15 MYTHS, MISTAKES, AND MISREPRESENTATIONS ABOUT THE DEUTEROCANON

© 2017 by Gary G. Michuta. All rights reserved.

Published by Nikaria Press

Livonia, Michigan

www.HandsOnApologetics.com

Printed in the United States of America

Library of Congress Cataloguing-in-Publication Data

Michuta, Gary G., 1964 -

15 Myths, Mistakes, and Misrepresentations about the Deuterocanon

ISBN-10: 0-9988399-4-9

ISBN-13: 978-0-9988399-4-3

Other Books and Resources by Gary Michuta

Hostile Witnesses: How The Historic Enemies of the Church Prove Christianity

The Case for the Deuterocanon: Evidence and Arguments

Making Sense of Mary

How to Wolf-Proof Your Kids: A Practical Guide To Keeping Your Kids Catholic

Why Catholic Bibles Are Bigger: The Untold Story of the Lost Books of the Protestant Bible

The Gospel According to James McCarthy: A Catholic Answer to James McCarthy's "The Gospel According to Rome"

CD SETS

Defending the Faith Series Volumes 1-5 (Is Salvation Guaranteed? / Is Sacred Tradition Necessary? / From Peter to Papacy / The Sacrifice of the Mass / Mary: Unveiling the Blessed Virgin's Role in God Plan of Redemption)

An Unexpected Calling / Does Romans Teach Justification Apart from Works? (Michuta - Kliewer) / The Claims of Christ and the Reliability of the Gospels / The Jehovah's Witnesses Explained: A Catholic Look at the Watchtower's History and Doctrine

www.HandsOnApologetics.com

www.GaryMichuta.com

Contents

INTRODUCTION 7

MYTH #1 THE JEWS ONLY ACCEPTED WRITINGS IN HEBREW 15

MYTH #2 THE ALEXANDRIAN CANON VERSUS THE PALESTINIAN CANON 17

MYTH #3 THE COUNCIL OF JAMNIA DECIDED WHICH BOOKS ARE SCRIPTURE 21

MYTH #4 TRENT'S "ARBITRARY" SELECTION 23

MYTH #5 NO HEBREW SCHOLARS AT TRENT 29

MISTAKE #1 THE NEW TESTAMENT IS SILENT IN REGARD TO THE DEUTEROCANON................................39

MISTAKE #2 PHILO'S REJECTION OF THE DEUTEROCANON 43

MISTAKE #3 THE ABSENCE AT QUMRAN OF A PESHER ON THE DEUTEROCANON 45

MISTAKE #4 THE GREEK CHURCH CHANGED ITS MIND ON THE DEUTEROCANON 47

MISTAKE #5 TRENT'S DECREE ON THE CANON PASSED WITH ONLY 44% OF THE VOTE..51

MISREPRESENTATION #1 THE NEW AMERICAN BIBLE'S "ADMISSION" ABOUT THE DEUTEROCANON................59

MISREPRESENTATION #2 QUMRAN'S SPECIAL PARCHMENT AND SCRIPT ARGUMENT..........................63

MISREPRESENTATION #3 JEROME FOLLOWED THE
MAJORITY OPINION WHEN HE REJECTED THE
DEUTEROCANON 77

MISREPRESENTATION #4 FLORENCE'S ACCEPTANCE
OF THE DEUTEROCANON BOLSTERED BELIEF IN
PURGATORY. 83

MISREPRESENTATION #5 THE NEW CATHOLIC
ENCYCLOPEDIA SAYS TRENT IS THE FIRST INFALLIBLE
DECREE ON THE CANON..89

INDEX...103

INTRODUCTION

One of the biggest issues that separate Catholics and Protestants is the Old Testament canon. While we share a majority of the Old Testament books, there are seven books (as well as sections in the books of Daniel and Esther) that Catholics and the Orthodox accept as inspired canonical Scripture, but that Protestants reject as human "Apocrypha." Catholics and the Orthodox call these books the "Deuterocanon."

Why Catholics and Protestants have two different Old Testaments has become a popular subject on the Internet. Unfortunately, however, a lot of erroneous information seems to get recycled over and over again on various non-Catholic blogs, websites, and social media platforms. Whether it is the allure of posting potentially damning information on Catholicism or the ease of copying and pasting others' material, it's out there for everyone to see. Many of these errors have been addressed in my two books on the Deuterocanon (Why Catholic Bibles Are Bigger: The Untold Story of the Lost Books of the Protestant Bible, 2nd ed. (Catholic Answers Press, 2017) and The Case for the Deuterocanon: Evidence and Argument (Nikaria Press, 2016)), but a few remain that didn't fit into the overall scope of either book. Nevertheless, they need to be debunked. Therefore, I decided to gather them together into this short book for those who do not have the time to run down the facts about these fanciful claims.

It should be noted at the outset that some individuals are more frequently mentioned in this book than others. This is entirely by accident. It's just that some individuals have written more extensively on the Deuterocanon (the "Apocrypha," as it is called by non-Catholics) than others, and even the best scholars occasionally make mistakes.

Let's begin by defining important terms, since our discussion will use terminology that isn't very common.

CANON

The word "canon" comes from the Greek word "kanon," which refers to a reed or a measuring rod. It was used in the New Testament and the early Church to mean a rule or a standard. Later in Church history, the word was applied to the contents of sacred Scripture. In this sense, the canon of Scripture is a list of inspired authoritative works.

DEUTEROCANON

What is the Deuterocanon? The Deuterocanon consists of seven Old Testament books (Sirach, Wisdom, Baruch, Tobit, Judith, and First and Second Maccabees) as well as some sections in the books of Esther and Daniel. Catholics call these books deuterocanonical (or "second canon") as distinguished from the Protocanon (the "first canon"), which consists of the books that Catholic, Orthodox, Protestants, and Jews hold in common.

APOCRYPHA

What is the Apocrypha? Protestants use this term for the Deuterocanon. Since they deny that the Deuterocanon is inspired canonical Scripture, they call it the "Apocrypha": that is, uninspired religious writings. Since it would be too cumbersome to call these books by both terms in this text, we will simply call them the deuterocanonical books.

INSPIRATION

We use the word "inspiration" today to mean something that is uplifting, motivating, or encouraging. It may even be used to suggest that a work is insightful, such as when someone says, "That was an inspired speech" or "That movie is inspired." In discussions about Scripture and the canon of Scripture, however, inspiration has a technical meaning that is unrelated to this. Inspiration means that God is the primary author of a given writing. The human author is the secondary author of Scripture, a person who was moved by God to write down only those things that God wished to be consigned to writing.

Now that we've covered the basics, we are ready to look at fifteen common and not so common myths, mistakes, and misrepresentations that you may have already stumbled across in blogs and Internet articles. For brevity's sake, I've included footnotes to both of my books for further reading. Enjoy!

MYTHS

What better way is there to begin a book such as this than with five of the most common and not-so-common myths about the Deuterocanon? "What are myths?" you may ask. For our purposes, we'll define a myth as an assertion or idea that lacks supporting evidence even though many people hold it to be true.

Some of these myths were once viable theories that provided simple answers to the questions of their day, but further research revealed that they were based on faulty information and that their solutions weren't really solutions at all. While the scholarly world moved on to greener pastures, many people continued to spread these myths, especially online.

These relics of the past aren't the only kinds of myths out there, however. There are also myths that masquerade as the arguments known as conspiracy theories. Where discarded theories are attractive because they provide simple solutions to complex problems, conspiracy theories are attractive because they use the reader's antagonism toward an idea or institution to obscure the fact that the theory has no supporting evidence. In this chapter, we will look at two such conspiracy myths that are aimed at making false and defamatory statements about the Council of Trent, which reaffirmed the Deuterocanon as Scripture after the Protestant Reformation.

These aren't the only myths circulating on the Internet concerning the Deuterocanon, but they are among the most common ones that haven't yet been debunked by either of my books.

MYTH #1 THE JEWS ONLY ACCEPTED WRITINGS IN HEBREW

Our first myth concerns the language of the Old Testament Scripture. It generally runs like this:

> When the Jews were discerning which books belonged in the Bible, they accepted only texts that were written in Hebrew, since it was the sacred language of God's People before the coming of Christ. The Deuterocanon, however, was written in Greek. Therefore, the Jews never considered the Deuterocanon to be a real candidate for sacred Scripture.

Although people state this point as if it really occurred, such was not the case. As we will see with the myth of the "council" of Jamnia, the Jews never actually gathered together as a group to decide which books were Scripture, much less say, "Let's reject any text that is not written in Hebrew." It didn't happen.

Since there is nothing in Scripture that states that all inspired Old Testament works must be written in Hebrew, how did this idea come about? The best answer seems to be that most people assume that the Hebrews spoke Hebrew, so it was therefore a special, sacred language. While it is true that Hebrew was used during a substantial part of sacred history, it wasn't the only language used by the Jews. God's People also spoke Aramaic and eventually Greek.

Could God inspire Scripture in languages other than Hebrew? We know that he did. For example, there are portions of the Old Testament that were inspired in Aramaic, not Hebrew (Genesis 31:47; Ezra 4:8-6, 18; 7:12-26; Jeremiah 10:11). He also inspired the Greek New Testament. If God can inspire the Greek New Testament, why couldn't he do the same in the Old Testament when the People of God spoke Greek as well?

Besides being baseless, the myth also errs in regard to the Deuterocanon. It claims that the Deuterocanon was originally written in Greek, but this is not true. It appears that the books of Sirach, Tobit, Judith, Baruch, and First Maccabees were originally written in Hebrew or Aramaic, not Greek. Only two deuterocanonical books – Wisdom and Second Maccabees – were originally written in Greek. This means that, even if the baseless claim that God could only inspire Old Testament Scripture in Hebrew were true, it would not disqualify the Deuterocanon as a whole because most of it was written in Hebrew or Aramaic.

MYTH #2 THE ALEXANDRIAN CANON VERSUS THE PALESTINIAN CANON

This myth originated in Protestant circles, but still circulates even among Catholics today. It is the "two-canon" myth, and it runs like this:

> There existed two different canons of Scripture in the first century. One canon was held by the Hebrew-speaking Jews in Palestine. These Jews were very conservative and only accepted books written in Hebrew. This "Palestinian canon" consisted of the same books that are found in the Protestant Old Testament. The Jews in Alexandria, however, had a different canon of Scripture. The Greek-speaking Jews of Alexandria were not as conservative as those in Palestine and were willing to accept books that were written in Greek. Their "Alexandrian canon" was larger than the canon of Palestine because they accepted the Hebrew protocanonical books as well as the Deuterocanon. Even though the "Palestinian canon" and the "Alexandrian canon" were both Jewish, they were not equally authoritative. Palestine was the center of Judaism. Therefore, the "Palestinian canon" is considered more authoritative and authentic than the "Alexandrian canon."

Protestant scholars were the first to propound the "two-canon" theory, doing so in the first decades of the eighteenth century. At the time, it seemed to provide an adequate explanation as to why an ancient Jewish Greek translation of the Old Testament known as the Septuagint included the Deuterocanon while the Hebrew Masoretic text did not. Language and location seemed to supply a key to unlock this question. As neat and tidy as the "two-canon" theory seemed to be, however, it was based on faulty information.

As more and more information became known about first-century Judaism, more and more of the "two-canon" theory began to unravel. Credit for its ultimate demise, however, should go to the Harvard biblical scholar A.C. Sundberg, whose doctoral thesis exposed the theory's unsubstantiated assumptions.

The main problem for the "two-canon" theory is its reliance on the use of language. First, it commits the same error as the myth above: namely, believing that the Deuterocanon was originally composed in Greek. Only two of the seven deuterocanonical books were written in Greek. The rest were written in Hebrew or Aramaic. Second, the sharp division between the Hebrew-speaking Palestinian Jews and the Greek-speaking Alexandrian Jews is unsubstantiated. We now know that Palestine (and Jerusalem) was just as Hellenized as any other city in the Middle East at this time. It was not uncommon for Jews to speak both Aramaic and Greek. Therefore, it is quite possible that synagogues with a large number of Greek-speaking Jews used the Greek Septuagint as their Scripture, which included the books of the Deuterocanon.[1]

---

[1] See "Septuagint 'Plus' is the Septuagint" in *The Case for the Deuterocanon: Evidence and Arguments* (Livonia, MI: Nikaria Press), 2015, 67-72.

Therefore, the Hebrew-speaking versus Greek-speaking element of the "two-canon" theory is entirely a thing of fiction.

Where the "two-canon theory" errs by using language to try to explain how Christians and Jews ended up with two different Old Testament canons, a better way to understand it is in terms of time. Christians inherited the collection of Old Testament Scriptures from Christ and His Apostles in the first century, and they continued to use it throughout their history. This "canon" included both the Protocanon and the Deuterocanon.[2] Rabbinical Judaism in the second Christian century adopted its own normative collection of Scripture, and this later collection did not include the Deuterocanon.[3] Both are Jewish and came from Judaea (Palestine)—but they came about at different times and from different sources.

Even though the old Palestinian versus Alexandrian theory was abandoned by scholars as far back as the 1950s, some still continue to argue it today.

---

[2] The thesis of *The Case for the Deuterocanon: Arguments and Evidence* is to show through several lines of argument that the Deuterocanon was part of the original collection of sacred works Christ and his apostles handed on to the Church.

[3] See *Why Catholic Bibles Are Bigger: The Untold Story of the Lost Books of the Protestant Bible*, 2nd edition (San Diego: Catholic Answers Press), 44-50; *The Case for the Deuterocanon*, 55-65.

MYTH #3 THE COUNCIL OF JAMNIA DECIDED WHICH BOOKS ARE SCRIPTURE

The "council" of Jamnia myth runs something like this:

> Around A.D. 100, rabbis gathered together in a council in the city of Jamnia to decide which books were Scripture and which ones were not. This authoritative council accepted only the protocanonical books and rejected the Deuterocanon.

The origin of the "council" in the Jamnia myth can be traced back to the Jewish philosopher Baruch Spinoza, who wrote in 1670 that the divisions of sacred books were made by the "concilium Pharisaeorum" ("council of Pharisees"). The Jewish historian Heinrich Graetz (1871) took Spinoza's words to mean that a "Synod" was called to rule on which books were to be accepted. Hence, the myth of the "council" of Jamnia was born. But did the rabbis meet in a council in Jamnia to decide the canon of Scripture?

In 1964, Jack P. Lewis debunked the "council" myth in an article for the Journal of Bible and Religion titled, "What Do We Mean By Jebneh?" The truth is that there never was a group of rabbis who met in A.D. 90 (some say A.D. 100) to issue a decree on the canon of Scripture. The city of Jamnia did host a rabbinical school or academy. The academy functioned as a center for learning and a Sanhedrin. Although it did host discussions about the sacredness of different books (including disputes about Ecclesiastes and Song of Songs), the academy at Jamnia never issued an official decree or list of the books of the Old Testament.[4] This is not to say that Jamnia played no role in the formation of the canon. Quite the contrary: it was under the auspices of the head rabbi at Jamnia, Rabbi Akiva ben Joseph, that a single normative Hebrew text was eventually adopted. Up until that time, the Jews used several different translations and versions of the Old Testament, most especially the Greek translation known as the Septuagint (or "Seventy"). It was under Akiva and sometime around A.D. 135 that a single Hebrew text, now known as the Masoretic text, became the official normative Scripture for rabbinical Judaism. The new normative collection did not include the Deuterocanon. Eventually, this one official text replaced both the Greek Septuagint and the other Hebrew texts in existence. Christians, however, continued to use the older collection of texts that included the Deuterocanon.

Therefore, there never was a "council" in the Christian sense of the term. Instead, Jamnia hosted a rabbinical school or academy that, over a period of time, did play a role in the formation of the rabbinical Bible.

---

[4] For more information about Jamnia and what role it did play, see *Why Catholic Bibles Are Bigger*, 44-50.

MYTH #4 TRENT'S "ARBITRARY" SELECTION

The Council of Trent (1545-1563) met to reaffirm aspects of the Catholic faith that Protestantism denied. At the fourth session (April 4, 1546), the Council reaffirmed the canon of Scripture, which included the Deuterocanon. Our next myth claims that Trent arbitrarily selected which books it would affirm or reject based on its own theological view. As Norman Geisler asserts in his book Roman Catholics and Evangelicals: Agreements and Disagreements:

> "Not all the Apocrypha was accepted at Trent. In fact, they arbitrarily accepted a book favoring their belief in prayers for the dead (2 Maccabees) and rejected one opposing such prayers (2 [4] Esdras; cf. 7:105). Thus Trent's acceptance of the Apocrypha was unfounded." (p. 172)

To make things simpler, we will call 2 [4] Esdras by its other name, the Apocalypse of Esdras. The myth states that the fathers at Trent cherry-picked only the books that were to their liking, so they affirmed Second Maccabees as Scripture because it supported prayers for the dead (i.e., purgatory), but rejected the Apocalypse of Esdras because it rejected prayers for the dead.

At first glance, this myth may seem plausible, but it has a problem: there is not a shred of evidence to support it. In fact, all of the available evidence speaks against it. Consider the following points.

First, the deliberations of the Council are public knowledge. The official *Acts of the Council* is available along with the various diaries and letters of its participants. We know how Trent's decisions came about, and it wasn't from arbitrarily picking and choosing books. Trent's decree on the canon essentially reproduces the same canon previously given by early councils like the councils of Hippo Regius (393), Carthage III (397), Carthage IV (419), and Florence (1442), as well as various papal pronouncements (i.e., Innocent I (405), Gelasius (r. 492-496), etc.).[5] All of these councils accepted Second Maccabees, and all of them omitted the Apocalypse of Esdras. Therefore, the books that Trent affirmed weren't arbitrary.

Moreover, the Apocalypse of Esdras doesn't contradict the Church's teachings on purgatory. The Apocalypse of Esdras 7:101-107 reads:

> "I answered and said, 'If I have found favor in your sight, show further to me, your servant, whether on the day of judgment the righteous will be able to intercede for the ungodly or to entreat the Most High for them—fathers for sons or sons for parents, brothers for brothers, relatives for their kindred, or friends for those who are most dear.' He answered me and said, 'Since you have found favor in my sight, I will show you this also. The day of judgment is decisive and displays to all the seal of truth. Just as now a father does not send his son, or a son his father, or a master his servant, or a friend his dearest friend, to be ill or sleep or eat or be healed in his place, so no one

---

[5] *Why Catholic Bibles Are Bigger* (2nd ed.), 130-133.

shall ever pray for another on that day, neither shall anyone lay a burden on another; for then all shall bear their own righteousness and unrighteousness."

A closer look at this text reveals that, although it does deny the efficacy of prayers for the dead, it doesn't contradict the Catholic understanding of purgatory. Here's why. The Apocalypse poses the question, "whether *on the day of judgment* the righteous will be able to intercede for the ungodly or to entreat the Most High for them" (emphasis added). The answer that is given is "no." However, Catholicism doesn't teach that prayers will be effective during or after the Final Judgment. On the contrary, it has been the Church's common understanding that the final sanctification of the righteous (i.e., those in purgatory) will be completed by the Final Judgment.[6] St. Augustine (354-430), for example, said:

"Whether we suffer temporary punishments in this life only, or in the life after death, or in both, the sufferings precede *that last, severe judgment.*" (*City of God*, 21, 13) (Emphasis added.)

Likewise, quoting Pope St. Gregory the Great (d. 604), the Catechism of the Catholic Church teaches:

"As for certain lesser faults, we must believe that, before the Final Judgment, there is a purifying

---

[6] According to Ludwig Ott, the teaching that "The purifying fire will not continue after the General Judgment," the common teaching of the Catholic Church (*sententia communis*) (*Fundamentals of Catholic Dogma* (Charlotte, NC: TAN books), 1992, 485).

fire" (CCC 1031, quoting St. Gregory the Great, Dial. 4, 39) (Emphasis added.)

Therefore, the Apocalypse of Esdras comments about the day of judgment; it does not contradict Catholic teaching, but instead actually supports it.

Furthermore, the passage concerns the question of interceding for the "ungodly" after they die. In regard to their fate, the Apocalypse answers that their fate is unalterable: "The day of judgment is decisive...for then all shall bear their own righteousness or unrighteousness." This also fits Catholic theology. Our prayers for the dead do not and cannot change the eternal destiny of our loved ones. If they die in mortal sin (i.e., in an ungodly state), they will be damned. No amount of prayers can save the ungodly from damnation. Likewise, if they die in God's grace, they are unalterably destined for glory in heaven. Prayers only assist in the final sanctification of those destined for heaven (i.e., those who die in godliness). Therefore, Second Maccabees and the Apocalypse of Esdras do not contradict each other as this myth suggests, since both texts are addressing different issues. 2 Maccabees 12:46 addresses the final sanctification of those who died in godliness:

> "But if he did this [offered prayers and contributed money for sacrifices] with a view to the splendid reward that awaits those who had gone to rest *in godliness*, it was a holy and pious thought." (Emphasis added.)

The Apocalypse of Esdras, however, addresses "whether on the day of judgment the righteous will be able to intercede *for the ungodly* or to entreat the Most High for them" (emphasis added), which is a

26

different issue. In regard to the effectiveness of prayers for the ungodly, the answer is "no." They will fall under the judgment of God, and no one can change their final condition.

Since the Apocalypse of Esdras neither contradicts Second Maccabees nor the Catholic understanding of purgatory/praying for the dead, it could hardly have been the reason why the Council of Trent affirmed Second Maccabees and not the Apocalypse of Esdras. The real reason—the one supported by all of the evidence—is that the Council of Trent affirmed the canon given by previous councils. None of these councils affirmed the Apocalypse of Esdras.

MYTH #5 NO HEBREW SCHOLARS AT TRENT

This myth, like the previous one, attempts to undermine the Council of Trent's canon (and approval of the Deuterocanon), only this one does so by claiming that the Council fathers were incompetent. The myth seems to have originated with the Protestant theologian J. B. Westcott and become popularized by the anti-Catholic author George Salmon (1819-1904), although it is possible that it may have originated earlier. Here is what Salmon wrote:

> "The great bulk of the bishops [at Trent] were Italian; of the rest the majority were Spanish; there were a couple from France, none from Germany, Switzerland, or the Northern countries. But a still worse account has to be given of the scholarship of its members. *None knew Hebrew; only a few knew Greek; there were even some whose knowledge of Latin was held in but low repute; not one had eminence as a learned divine.* Westcott's summing-up of the case is completely justified. 'This fatal decree in which the Council, harassed by the fear of lay critics and 'grammarians,' gave a new aspect to the whole question of the Canon, was ratified by fifty-three prelates, *among whom there was not one German, not one scholar distinguished by historical learning, not one who was fitted by special study for the examination of a subject* in which the truth could only be determined by the voice of

antiquity. How completely the decision was opposed to the spirit and letter of the original judgments of the Greek and Latin Churches; how far it was at variance, in the doctrinal equalization of the disputed and acknowledged books of the Old Testament, with the tradition of the West; how absolutely unprecedented was the conversion of an ecclesiastical usage into an article of belief, will be seen from the evidence which has been already adduced.'" (George Salmon, General Introduction, The Holy Bible, ed. Wace, The Apocrypha, vol. 1, xxxiv, quoting Westcott's Bible in the Church, 257) (Emphasis added.)

Perhaps the single best response to Salmon's and Westcott's calumnies came by way of an editorial in the *Dublin Review*:

"This is certainly most unjust. Jansen, Lippomani, Salmeron, Jerome Oleaster, [and] Foreiro were good Hebrew scholars, and the authors of learned commentaries on parts of the Old Testament. Cardinals Cervini and Seripando were men of learning and eminence. The Dominican De Soto, to mention no other, was certainly a learned divine. Dr. Salmon surely forgets that nearly all the bishops and theologians present had passed through universities, where, in accordance with the decree of Clement V, from the middle of the fourteenth century, Greek, Hebrew, and Chaldee [Aramaic] had been publicly taught. It is true that the German bishops were not present at the fourth session, but Dr. Salmon forgets that their opinion, and that of other learned men, was carefully ascertained by letter. Though the number of the Fathers in the fourth session did not exceed fifty-three, their decree was afterwards confirmed by the whole Council, and accepted by numerous provincial councils all over the Catholic world. Dr. Salmon insinuates that 'controversial inducements' led to the recognition of the Apocrypha. It is far more likely that the Reformers were influenced by such inducements in their rejection. For Reuss, no friendly witness, says, 'The Apocrypha were disliked, because Catholic dogmas were disliked; and the weakness of the arguments against them was only equaled by the violence with which they were put forward'" ("Notices of Books" in the *Dublin Review*, Third Series, vol. 21, January-April, 1889, 232).

Since the *Dublin Review* packs a lot of information into a few short paragraphs, let's unpack its major points.

Salmon's claim that "None knew Hebrew; only a few knew Greek" at the Council of Trent is directly contradicted by the facts. Francisco Foreiro (1523-1581), for example, wrote a commentary on Isaiah using the Hebrew text. He also examines the Hebrew text in his other commentaries on the books of Job, Psalms, and the Wisdom literature. Aloysii Lippomani (1500-1559) likewise wrote commentaries on Genesis and Exodus utilizing both Greek and Hebrew. The same can be said of Jerome Oleaster (d. 1563), who was proficient in Hebrew and Greek and wrote commentaries on the Pentateuch. Alphonsus Salmeron (1515-1585) produced several commentaries on the New Testament (on the Gospels, Acts, and four Pauline epistles); however, he was most famous for his knowledge of Hebrew. All of these council fathers not only knew Hebrew, but were especially adept at it.

In addition to these prestigious scholars, all of the fathers at Trent were educated either at a university or in a monastery, and both of these institutions gave instruction on ancient languages. As the editor noted, Pope Clement V (1305-1314) at the council of Vienne (1312) authorized that chairs be established at universities for the study of the Hebrew language. Pope John XXII (1316-1334) later published the Vienne decree as part of the Code of Canon Law recommending that the major universities establish chairs in Hebrew, Greek, Aramaic, and Arabic. All of these languages, except Arabic, eventually became part and parcel of a university education. By the time of St. John Fisher (1469-1535), instruction in ancient languages had become so integrated into university life that St. John's College had a rule that students could converse with each other in the dining hall only in Hebrew, Arabic, Aramaic, Greek, or Latin. Therefore, the university-educated council fathers most certainly learned at least Hebrew and Greek. As for those who were educated in their religious orders, many religious orders had missions in the East. As a result, they required their members to be fluent in Eastern languages. In fact, the monasteries were teaching ancient languages long before they were taught at many universities. Therefore, Salmon's claim that none of the council fathers knew Hebrew is simply ludicrous.

The *Dublin Review* easily dispatched the charge that Trent was also devoid of "learned divines." If any doubt persists, we can also point to the fact that, in addition to the learned theologians mentioned by the editorial, there was also a panel of theological consultants who the Council fathers could consult when needed. The number of consultants varies according to the source, but the Catholic Encyclopedia puts the number of this panel at forty-two theologians and nine canonists (*Catholic Encyclopedia* (New York: Catholic Encyclopedia Press), 1917, vol. 15, 31).

Of course, none of Salmon's or Westcott's charges are really relevant to the question of the canon of Scripture. Salmon and Westcott seem to believe that the canon of Scripture was an open question and that the Council needed to construct a biblical canon from scratch, hence the need for the most learned Hebraists and theologians. However, no one is competent to construct a biblical canon because the canon isn't something that humans put together. In a real sense, God constructs that canon by inspiring a certain number of books. These books were given by Christ and his apostles to the Church. Therefore, the canon is (objectively speaking) something to be received, not decided upon. The Council's job – indeed any council's job – is to faithfully pass on and protect what has already been received. Trent undoubtedly had all of the intellectual firepower that Salmon and Westcott denied, but even if their charges were true and Trent was filled with non-scholarly types, the Council could still do its job by faithfully passing on what had already been decided by previous councils. Salmon and Westcott seem to have missed this very fundamental point.

MISTAKES

In the last section, we looked at five commonly propounded myths about the Deuterocanon. We will now turn our attention to mistakes. These mistakes, like the myths above, are frequently copied and pasted on the Internet as indisputable facts. Sadly, all of these mistakes could have been avoided had a little more attention been given to the details.

The first three mistakes commit the same fundamental blunder in three different ways, namely that they attempt to turn the absence of evidence into positive evidence against the Deuterocanon. The best way to correct such a blunder is to get a bird's eye view of all of the data and expose just how insignificant the absence of evidence really is. The problem is that few people have the time or the inclination to do the painstaking work of gathering such data, so the point is usually just conceded. In this section, we've supplied the data for you so that you'll be able to clear up these mistaken arguments without much effort.

The remaining blunders are also the result of inattention to detail. Most people who are already inclined to dismiss the Deuterocanon as uninspired "Apocrypha" will accept these claims at face value simply because of the prestige of the authors who made them. Since their topics are not very well-known, most people have no reason to suspect that they are wrong.

MISTAKE #1 THE NEW TESTAMENT IS SILENT IN REGARD TO THE DEUTEROCANON

Of all the myths, mistakes, and misrepresentations about the Deuterocanon, this one is made most frequently. It says:

> The New Testament quotes from practically every book in the Old Testament, but it never makes a clear, definite quotation from the Deuterocanon. Therefore, the Deuterocanon was not considered Scripture by Jesus, his apostles, or the writers of the New Testament.

At first glance this mistake may appear to be more of a myth – as in, "the myth of the Apocrypha-less New Testament" – but there is some truth to the claim. It's true that the New Testament does not quote the Deuterocanon in a clear and definite manner. However, the claim is mistaken on a number of other points.

First, it doesn't explain why the lack of a clear and direct quotation is a make-or-break condition for canonicity. In other words, the restriction seems to be arbitrary. After all, who said that unless the New Testament clearly and definitely quotes a book, it can't be considered Scripture? Scripture doesn't teach this. Moreover, if a clear and definite quotation really is the sine qua non for being Scripture, we have a problem. The New Testament doesn't make a clear and definite quotation from the books of Ruth, First and Second Chronicles, Ezra, Esther, Song of Songs, Ecclesiastes, Lamentations, Ezekiel, or Daniel, either. Aren't they considered Scripture?

Second, why restrict the evidence to only clear and direct quotations? The New Testament uses the Old Testament in a number of different ways besides direct quotations. Sometimes it paraphrases Old Testament passages. Other times, it alludes to a text or references something in it. Don't these items also have evidentiary weight? Before you answer that question, consider the book of Jonah. What's interesting about the book of Jonah is that the New Testament never quotes it, yet you won't find Jonah listed as a book that the New Testament never quotes. Pretty strange, isn't it? The reason why is that, although Jonah is never directly quoted, it is referenced by Jesus in the New Testament (Matthew 12:39-42, 16:1-4; Luke 11:29-32). Therefore, these references count as an affirmation of Jonah. If a reference is as good as a direct quote to approve the book of Jonah, why can't the references to the Deuterocanon (e.g., Hebrews 11:35) also count as evidence for the Deuterocanon? Clearly, the insistence of a clear and direct quotation as evidence to affirm a book as Scripture is simply too restrictive.

Instead of looking only at explicit quotes, what needs to be done is to look at all of the evidence (quotations, allusions, references, etc.) and see what it has to tell us about the inspired status of the Deuterocanon. The results of such a study will reveal that the New Testament does indeed use the Deuterocanon as inspired Scripture. [7]

WHAT ABOUT FORMAL QUOTES?

It's funny to see how many times the claim that the New Testament never clearly and directly quotes the Deuterocanon is followed by the claim that the New Testament never "formally quotes" the Deuterocanon, either. If there are no "clear and direct" quotations, of course there wouldn't be any formal quotations. Be that as it may, here is how the "formal quote" mistake is commonly given:

The New Testament never formally quotes the Deuterocanon with such words as "The Scripture says," "It is written," or "Thus says the Lord." Even though the New Testament quotes practically every protocanonical

---

[7] See *Why Catholic Bibles are Bigger*, 30-42, also *The Case for the Deuterocanon*, 1-37.

book with these formal introductions, the Deuterocanon is not once quoted in such an authoritative way.

The mistake here is one of exaggeration. If you broke down how many books are quoted by these introductory formulas, you'll find that the statement that "practically every protocanonical book" is quoted is a bit of a stretch. Let's look at each of the three formal introductions. Using the standard Nestle-Aland Greek New Testament (27th edition), let's discover how many times these formal introductions are used and how many books are quoted using these introductions.

"The Scripture says" (Greek, *eipen hē graphē*) occurs nine times in the NA27.[8] It introduces quotes from the books of Genesis (twice), Psalms, Zechariah, Exodus, Isaiah, 1 Kings, and Deuteronomy. James 4:5 also uses this introduction to formally quote a book that cannot be identified. Therefore, only seven books of the Protestant Bible (plus one unknown book) are quoted with this introduction.

"As it is written" (Greek, *gegraptai*) occurs sixty-nine times in the NA27.[9] It introduces quotes from Micah, Deuteronomy (eleven times), Psalms (ten times), Malachi (four times), Isaiah (sixteen times), Zechariah (three times), Exodus (four times), Amos (twice), Habakkuk, Genesis (twice), 2 Samuel, Jeremiah, Job, and Leviticus. Therefore, these sixty-seven formal quotations cover only fourteen books of the Protestant Old Testament.

---

[8] John 19:28, 37; Romans 4:3, 9:17, 10:11, 11:2; Galatians 4:30; 1 Timothy 5:18, James 4:5.

[9] Matthew 2:5, 4:4, 6, 7, 10, 11:10, 21:13, 26:24, 31; Mark 1:2, 7:6, 9:12, 13, 11:17, 14:21, 27; Luke 2:23, 3:4, 4:4, 8, 10, 7:27, 10:26, 19:46, 24:46; John 8:17, 20:31; Acts 1:20, 7:42, 13:33, 15:15, 23:5; Romans 1:17, 2:24, 3:4, 10-11, 4:17, 8:36, 9:12-13, 33; 10:15, 11:8, 26-27, 12:19, 14:11, 15:3, 9, 21; 1 Corinthians 1:19, 31, 2:9, 3:19, 4:6, 9:9, 10:7, 14:21, 15:45; 2 Corinthians 8:15, 9:9; Galatians 3:10, 13, 4:22, 27; Hebrews 10:7; 1 Peter 1:16; Revelation 13:8, 17:8. [This includes "*gegrammenon*" used in John 6:31, 45].

"Thus says the Lord" (Greek, *legei kyrios*) occurs eleven times in the NA27.[10] It introduces quotes from the books of Isaiah (five or six times), Amos, Deuteronomy (or Psalms), either 2 Samuel or Jeremiah (three times), and Exodus. Therefore, these eleven instances reference, at the most, only seven books of the Protestant Old Testament.[11]

When all three formal introductions are combined and the duplicates discarded, a sum total of only fifteen Old Testament books receive one or more of these formal quotations. This means that twenty-four books of the Protestant Old Testament are never formally quoted with these introductions. As you can see, there certainly are a lot of formal quotations in the New Testament, but only from a few books. Moreover, even if the New Testament did formally quote the Deuterocanon, critics would be quick to point out that such a formal quotation really means nothing, since James 2:23 formally quotes an unknown work with the introduction "the Scripture says" (Greek, *hē graphē hē legousa*). Therefore, the presence or absence of a formal quote really isn't a make-or-break issue for determining whether the New Testament is considered a book to be inspired. All of the data needs to be considered.

---

[10] Acts 7:50, 15:18; Romans 12:19, 14:11, 1 Corinthians 14:21; 2 Corinthians 6:17; 8:18; Hebrews 8:8, 9, 10, 10:16; Revelation 1:8.
[11] Matthew 26:24, Mark 9:12, 13, 14:21, Luke 24:46, John 20:31, 1 Corinthians 4:6, Revelation 13:8 and 17:8 do not introduce a formal quotation.

MISTAKE #2 PHILO'S REJECTION OF THE DEUTEROCANON

Another common mistake concerns the first-century Jewish philosopher and author Philo of Alexandria (25 BC – A.D. 50). Like the "no quotation" mistake, it, too, attempts to turn Philo's silence on the Deuterocanon into evidence that he rejected it. The mistake runs like this:

> Philo of Alexandria wrote a lot of books in which he gave numerous quotations from the Old Testament. He makes so many quotations, in fact, that he practically quotes from every book in the Old Testament, yet he never quotes the Deuterocanon. Given that he makes such a vast amount of quotations, Philo's silence practically screams out for an explanation, and that explanation is that he did not consider the Deuterocanon to be Scripture.

This mistake claims that, although it is an argument from silence, the sheer quantity of Philo's Old Testament quotation is sufficient to turn the absence of a deuterocanonical quote into actual evidence for a rejection. But does Philo's silence really "scream out" for such an explanation?

There is no doubt that Philo does indeed make an enormous number of quotations. It's impossible to get an exact figure, but there seem to be around 2,050 Old Testament quotations in all. Wow! That's a lot of quotes! Before you start hearing the silence scream, however, a little more has to be said about these quotes. If you break down this number a little further, you'll find that, out of the 2,050 quotations Philo makes in his writings, only 50 come from books outside of the Torah or Pentateuch (i.e., Genesis, Exodus, Leviticus, Numbers, and Deuteronomy).[12] Yes, you've read that correctly. Around 2,000 quotes come from the Torah! That means that only 2.439% of his quotations come from books outside of the Pentateuch. Given these figures, it shouldn't surprise anyone that Philo also doesn't quote from the books of Ruth, Esther, Ecclesiastes, Song of Songs, Lamentations, Ezekiel, and Daniel.

Given the relatively few times that Philo quotes from books outside of the Torah, it would be reasonable to expect Philo to be silent on the Deuterocanon, just as he's silent in regards to several other books of the Old Testament. There's no screaming here.

---

[12] Sid Leiman, *The Canonization of the Hebrew Scripture: The Talmudic and Midrashic Evidence* (Hamden, Conn.: Archon), 1976, 31, 151 FN 146.

MISTAKE #3 THE ABSENCE AT QUMRAN OF A PESHER ON THE DEUTEROCANON

We've already looked at the mistaken argument regarding the silence on the Deuterocanon in the New Testament and the writings of Philo of Alexandria. Our next claim deals with the supposed silence of the Dead Sea Scrolls. It runs:

> The Jews at Qumran (the place where the Dead Sea Scrolls were discovered) wrote commentaries (called "pesher," plural "pesherim") on the books of Scripture. However, there were no commentaries (i.e., pesherim) written for any deuterocanonical book. Therefore, the Jews at Qumran must have considered the Deuterocanon to be Apocrypha.

That seems like a pretty hefty claim. No deuterocanonical commentaries? Clearly, the community at Qumran must not have held the Deuterocanon to be equal to the protocanonical books – or did they?

Like the mistakes explored above, this mistake is exposed when all of the data is revealed. Once this is done, it becomes clear that the absence of a pesher document hardly constitutes a rejection. Here is why.

There were only fifteen commentaries (pesherim) discovered at Qumran. They include commentaries on the following books: Isaiah (4Q161, 4Q162, 4Q163, 4Q164, 4Q165), Psalms (1Q16, 4Q171, 4Q173), and five of the minor Prophets (Habakkuk

(1QpHab), Micah (1Q14), Zephaniah (1Q15, 4Q170), Hosea (4Q166, 4Q167), and Nahum (4Q169)). In total, only seven of the thirty-nine protocanonical books of the Old Testament received a commentary (pesher) at Qumran. Given that so few canonical books actually received a pesher, the absence of a deuterocanonical pesher really isn't that odd.

It's true that there may have been more commentaries that were written but didn't survive the ages. Despite this, a good argument is based on evidence that is available, not evidence that is not available. The evidence that we do have shows that it was a rare privilege for any book to receive a pesher at Qumran. Therefore, the absence of a deuterocanonical pesher is so insignificant that it's a point hardly worth making.

MISTAKE #4 THE GREEK CHURCH CHANGED ITS MIND ON THE DEUTEROCANON

Our next mistake can be traced back to an article in Dr. Norman Geisler's *Baker Encyclopedia of Christian Apologetics* on the "Apocrypha, Old and New Testament." The error has subsequently been repeated on the Internet.

Under the heading "Acceptance of the Orthodox Church," Geisler states:

> "The Greek church has not always accepted the Apocrypha, nor is its present position unequivocal. At the synods of Constantinople (1638), Jaffa (1642), and Jerusalem (1672) these books were declared canonical. But even as late as 1839 their Larger Catechism expressly omitted the Apocrypha on the grounds that they did not exist in the Hebrew Bible."[13]

The root of this mistake is a misunderstanding about the nature of Eastern Orthodoxy. The "Orthodox Church" is not one single Church, but several autocephalous Churches (i.e., Greek, Russian, Romanian, etc.). Being autocephalous means that a Church is not subject to the authority of an external patriarch, which makes it largely autonomous. Therefore, what applies to one Orthodox

---

[13] Norman L. Geisler, *Baker Encyclopedia of Christian Apologetics* (Grand Rapids, MI: Baker Books), 1999, 30-31.

Church may not apply to another. Geisler seems to have forgotten this.

After correctly stating that there were three Greek Orthodox synods that affirmed the Deuterocanon as Scripture (Constantinople, Jaffa, and Jerusalem), he errs by stating that "their Larger Catechism..." (emphasis added) omits the so-called "Apocrypha." The word "their" in this context refers to the Greek Orthodox Church that was just previously mentioned. However, the Larger Catechism is not a catechism of the Greek Orthodox Church. The Larger Catechism (1839)–also known as the Catechism of St. Philaret (Drozdov) of Moscow–is a catechism of the Russian Orthodox Church, a different autocephalous entity. Therefore, Geisler's statement that "The Greek church has not always accepted the Apocrypha, nor is its present position unequivocal" really isn't true. The Russian Orthodox Church may have expressed doubts via the Larger Catechism, but the Greek Orthodox Church did not.

Here is the backstory. Early in the 1600s, Protestant Calvinists from Europe attempted to persuade the Orthodox to embrace Calvinism. Their efforts produced mixed results. The greatest achievement was the partial conversion of Cyril Lucaris, the Patriarch of Constantinople, along with various members of the Russian Orthodox Church. When Cyril began to impose his new Calvinist views about the Deuterocanon and other issues, however, he met with resistance. Three local synods were convened, and they reaffirmed the Deuterocanon as sacred Scripture (as Geisler mentions). Outside of the actions of Cyril Lucaris, the Greeks never adopted the Protestant canon.

The Russian Orthodox Church was different. Although it was also influenced by Protestant Calvinists on the canon, it took a much longer time before it returned back to the ancient canon. The Larger Catechism (1839) does indeed present the Calvinist position.[14] However, the Russian Orthodox Church has since moved back in union with the Greek Orthodox Church in regard to the canon, although it still holds the Larger Catechism in high esteem because it was written by a saint.

Is this a sign of indecision on the part of the Orthodoxy? It's clear that the Protestant canon was not part of the historic Orthodox faith. Despite Calvinist missionary efforts to the contrary, the Orthodox position still affirms the Deuterocanon as inspired Scripture.

---

[14] Questions 31-35.

MISTAKE #5 TRENT'S DECREE ON THE CANON PASSED WITH ONLY 44% OF THE VOTE

Even the best scholars occasionally make mistakes. Our next mistake can be traced back to a brilliant Protestant scholar named Bruce M. Metzger. In his work *The New Testament Canon: It's Origin, Development, and Significance*, he wrote the following about the Council of Trent:

> "Finally on 8 April 1546 by a vote of 24 to 15, with 16 abstentions, the Council issued a decree (*De Canonicis Scripturis*) in which, for the first time in the history of the Church, the question of the contents of the Bible was made an absolute article of faith and confirmed by an anathema."[15]

If you convert these votes to percentages, it comes out to 44% approved and 27% against with 29% abstaining—not very impressive numbers for something as important as the canon of Scripture. But did Trent really pass its decree by such small numbers?

Metzger's quote, quite frankly, is a mess. The decree concerning the Canonical Scriptures (*De Canonicis Scripturis*) was indeed ratified on April 8, 1546, by the General Council, but it was approved unanimously (*Concilium Tridentinum*, vol. 5, 92).

---

[15] Bruce M. Metzger, *The New Testament Canon: It's Origin, Development, and Significance* (Oxford: Clarendon), 1987, 246.

If this is so, where did Metzger come up with the voting totals of twenty-four to fifteen with sixteen abstentions? As it turns out, these voting totals didn't come from the ratification that took place on April 8th, but from another vote that took place earlier on February 15 of the same year. This vote obviously wasn't the ratification of the decree, but the response to a question posed to the council fathers about how the decree was to be framed.

On February 15, two questions were posed: "Should all of the books be approved that were approved at the Council of Florence?" and "Should an anathema be added to the decree?" Of the two questions, the first is the most important, since it frames the canon itself. To this question, all answered "placet" ("yes"). In regards to the second question about adding an *anathema*, twenty-four fathers responded in favor of adding an *anathema*, while fifteen fathers voted against its addition, with the rest abstaining (Concilium Tridentinum, vol. 5, 10).[16] Metzger transposed the voting totals of this preliminary vote to the final ratification of the decree, which took place a few months later on April 8. By doing so, he makes it appear as though the decree concerning the Canonical Scriptures squeaked through the Council with only a minority of fathers in favor, when in fact it was adopted unanimously.

Metzger makes a second blunder as well. He seems to claim that the addition of the *anathema* made Trent's canon an "absolute" article of faith. One wonders what he means by an "absolute article of faith," since all of the articles of faith are "absolute" in the sense that they are true and binding; they differ only in terms of the solemnity in which they are proposed. The problem, for Metzger, is

---

[16] An anathema is a disciplinary measure that means that any Catholic holding a contrary view could be subject to the penalty prescribed by the Canon Law of the Church, namely excommunication.

that the *anathema* doesn't pertain to doctrine per se, but to discipline. It warns the faithful that to deny this proposition would make them liable to a canonical penalty. Even if Trent's decree did not have an *anathema*, however, its authority as an article of faith would remain unchanged, since it had already been defined as an "absolute article of faith" centuries before Trent convened.

Therefore, Metzger's mistake about what the minority voting tally represented and its implications in terms of making the canon an "absolute article of the faith" gives a distorted view of what the Council fathers really thought about the decree on canon. Both the adoption of the canon as given by Florence and the final approval of the entire decree were unanimously approved. The addition of the *anathema* did receive some opposition (and indifference) by the Council fathers, but, as stated above, the *anathema* had nothing to do with making the canon an article of faith.

MISREPRESENTATIONS

We've now arrived at our third and final category, the misrepresentations. This is by far the most difficult fallacy to detect and the most potentially explosive topic to address. A misrepresentation occurs when an author gives his readers a false impression of what a source actually says. This is why misrepresentations are difficult to detect: the reader has access to the source material and takes the time to compare it with what the author says or unless the quote itself seems odd, few people (if any) will notice that a misrepresentation has occurred.

Exposing misrepresentations can also be potentially explosive, since most people assume that all misrepresentations are made intentionally or due to malice, which isn't necessarily the case. There are several other reasons why someone might misrepresent something. For example, they may not have understood their subject very well, or they may have suffered from inattention to detail or a lack of healthy skepticism about what they'd previously heard on the subject.

It is not our job to judge such things, though. The purpose of this book is simply to help clear up these misrepresentations and set the record straight.

MISREPRESENTATION #1 THE NEW AMERICAN BIBLE'S "ADMISSION" ABOUT THE DEUTEROCANON

Our first misrepresentation comes from Norman Geisler's "Apocrypha, Old and New Testaments" article in the *Baker Encyclopedia of Christian Apologetics*, which reads:

> "Even notes in the currently used Roman Catholic New American Bible (NAB) make the revealing admission that the Apocrypha are 'Religious books used by both Jews and Christians which were not included in the collection of inspired writing.' Instead, they '...were introduced rather late into the collection of the Bible. Catholics call them 'deuterocanonical' (second canon) books' (NAB, 413)."[17]

Geisler's version, however, misrepresents what the New American Bible dictionary actually says. The article that Geisler only partially quotes reads as follows:

> "APOCRYPHA. Religious books used by both Jews and Christians which were not included in the collection of inspired writings. In the Protestant Church, this term designates the books of Tobit, Judith, Maccabees, Wisdom, Baruch, and Ecclesiasticus, which were introduced rather

---

[17] As quoted in Norman Geisler's article "Apocrypha, Old and New Testaments" in *the Baker Encyclopedia of Christian Apologetics*, 29.

late into the collection of the Bible. Catholics call them 'deuterocanonical' books."[18]

As Geisler himself notes at the beginning of his encyclopedia article, Roman Catholics and the Orthodox do not use the term "Apocrypha," but " prefer to call them 'deuterocanonical,' or books of 'the second canon.'"[19] The word "Apocrypha" denotes human writings, and since Catholics and the Orthodox believe these books to be inspired and canonical Scripture, "Apocrypha" isn't really a fitting name. Therefore, when the Catholic New American Bible dictionary defines "Apocrypha," it is not referring to the Deuterocanon, but to a group of books that are human religious writings like the *Book of Enoch*, the *Assumption of Moses*, or the *Gospel of Mary*, etc. It is here that Geisler's misrepresentation occurs.

Geisler quotes the dictionary in such a way as to make it seem as though it is saying that the Deuterocanon is human Apocrypha.

After correctly quoting the first line of the definition, Geisler omits the very next line, which states that the title "Apocrypha" is used in "the Protestant Church" for the deuterocanonical books. Had he included this line, his readers would have been informed that the dictionary's definition did not include the Deuterocanon, which is precisely the opposite of what Geisler claims the dictionary admits. Even worse, he inserts his own words "Instead they" between the end of the first line (which speaks about true apocrypha) and the last half of the second line, thus giving the impression that the

---

[18] For those who wish to look up the original text, it is found in the *Saint Joseph Edition of the New American Bible* (Catholic Book Publishing Co.: New York), 1991 on page 412, not page 413.
[19] *"Apocrypha, Old and New Testaments,"* 28.

article was saying that Catholics call the "[r]eligious books used by both Jews and Christians which were not included in the collection of inspired writing" the Deuterocanon.

What Geisler styles as a "revealing admission" is nothing more than a misrepresentation created by some clever editing.

MISREPRESENTATION #2 QUMRAN'S SPECIAL PARCHMENT AND SCRIPT ARGUMENT

It was difficult to classify this item because it appears at first glance to be a myth but, upon further investigation, turns out to be a misrepresentation. The misrepresentation asserts that the Jews in Qumran (where the Dead Sea Scrolls were discovered) used a special parchment and wrote in a special script when they copied canonical Scripture. As Norman Geisler writes:

> "...[that] only canonical books, not the Apocrypha, were found in the special parchment and script indicates that the Qumran community did not view the apocryphal books as canonical. The noted scholar on the Dead Sea Scrolls, Millar Burroughs [sic], concluded: 'There is no reason to think that any of these works were venerated as Sacred Scripture.'"[20]

What exactly is this "special script" and "special parchment?" Geisler doesn't say. Moreover, it's odd that none of the Scroll specialists seem to be aware of this special biblical format. On the contrary, most scholars who specialize in Dead Sea Scroll research affirm that the Jews at Qumran accepted a larger canon that may have included the deuterocanonical books of Sirach and Tobit. If

---

[20] Norman Geisler, *Roman Catholics and Evangelicals: Agreements and Differences*, co-authored by Ralph MacKenzie (Grand Rapids, MI: Baker Publishing Group), 1995, 165.

the special script and parchment really did give such an unmistakable demarcation between the sacred and profane texts, how is it that the experts seem to have missed it? To answer this question, we need to dig deeper into the claim.

A "SPECIAL" PARCHMENT AND SCRIPT?

Was there a "special parchment" used exclusively for biblical texts? There were only three types of materials used at Qumran: papyrus, parchment (leather), and copper. Copper is the rarest; it is only used for one scroll, and that scroll contains no biblical material. Therefore, copper can be crossed off as an answer. What about the other two types of material? Qumran yielded copies of biblical texts in both papyrus and parchment, although most biblical texts tend to be written on parchment. Could parchment or leather be the "special parchment" mentioned by Geisler?

Since two of the deuterocanonical fragments at Qumran were written on parchment – more specifically, Sirach (2Q18) is written on parchment and Tobit (4Q197-200) is written on papyrus and parchment – parchment (leather) can't be the "special parchment" either.

THE SPECIAL HEBREW SCRIPT

What about the use of a special Hebrew script? Qumran's Hebrew texts are written in either square script or paleo-Hebrew.[21]

Both protocanonical and deuterocanonical texts are written in square script. Only a few, fifteen to be exact, are written with paleo-Hebrew script. Most of these come from the Pentateuch

---

[21] There also is a special Qumran Hebrew, but this doesn't affect our discussion.

(1Q3, 2Q5, 4Q11, 4Q12, 4Q22, 4Q45, 4Q46, 4Q101, 6Q1, 6Q2, and 11Q1), and one comes from Job (4Q101). There is also a paleo-Hebrew fragment from a work similar to the book of Joshua called 4Q paleo paraJoshua (4Q123), which can best be described as a paraphrase of Joshua 21.

Scholars are still debating whether this fragment comes from a re-written book of Joshua known as the *Apocryphon of Joshua* or a variant of the canonical book of Joshua. Therefore, the jury is still out as to whether this fragment can be classified as a biblical text.

There are also three other fragments (4Q124, 4Q125, 11Q22) that have eluded identification. Therefore, it is still an open question whether paleo-Hebrew was used exclusively for biblical texts. If paleo-Hebrew was this "special Hebrew script," it could hardly function as an indicator for canonicity, since it would only affirm the Pentateuch, Job, and possibly Joshua. Therefore, there doesn't seem to be a special script used that would provide a clear demarcation between the canonical and noncanonical texts at Qumran.

But if there is no special parchment and no special script, how could Geisler claim that there was?

FINDING THE SOURCE

Geisler makes the same point in several of his works, so maybe they will provide us with clues regarding what he is talking about. In an article in the *Baker Encyclopedia of Christian Apologetics*, he essentially repeats what he said in the Roman Catholics and Evangelicals book:

"...[that] only canonical books were found in the special parchment and script indicates that the Apocryphal books were not viewed as canonical by the Qumran community. Menahem Mansoor lists the following fragments of the Apocrypha and Pseudepigrapha: Tobit, in Hebrew and Aramaic; Enoch in Aramaic; Jubilees in Hebrew; Testament of Levi and Naphtali, in Aramaic; Apocryphal Daniel literature, in Hebrew and Aramaic, and Psalms of Joshua (Mansoor, 203). The noted scholar on the Dead Sea Scrolls, Millar Burroughs [sic], concluded: 'There is no reason to think that any of these works were venerated as Sacred Scripture' (Burroughs [sic], 178)."

The same is repeated in a slightly different fashion in his *Popular Handbook of Archaeology and the Bible*, co-authored by Joseph Holden (Baker Academic, 2013):

"Only the canonical books were found, written on special parchment in the sacred script. Based on the finding at Qumran, the Apocrypha was not viewed as canonical by the Qumran community" (p. 90).

However, the book *To Understand the Bible Look for Jesus: The Bible Student's Guide to the Bible's Central Theme* (Wipf & Stock Pub, Reprint 2002) provides a little more information in a footnote:

"Even the Messianic cult at Qumran possessed Apocryphal books but apparently did not esteem

66

them of equal value with the sacred Scriptures. Millar Burrows, More Light on the Dead Sea Scrolls (New York: Viking, 1958), p. 178 says of the Apocrypha, 'There is no reason to think that any of these works were venerated as Sacred Scripture.' Scholars cite several different lines of evidence for viewing the Apocrypha as noncanonical in Qumran: (1) the absence of any commentaries on the Apocryphal books, (2) the failure to find any Apocryphal books written on the more valuable writing materials like parchment, (3) and even the failure to find any Apocryphal books written in the special (taller) script, as were the canonical books." (p. 23, FN 1)

Finally, here are some clues! The Burrows quotation (with his name spelled correctly this time) is given followed by a bit of a more descriptive account of what constitutes the special writing material and script. The "canonical" texts are said to be "written on the more valuable writing materials like parchment" and the special script is describes as being "taller" (apparently in comparison to the "shorter" script used for profane sources). The most important clue, however, is the placement of the Burrows quotation. Could it be that Geisler got his information from Burrows?

"MORE LIGHT" ON THE SPECIAL SCRIPT

Millar Burrows' *More Light on the Dead Sea Scrolls* is no longer in print, but used copies are available online. If you pick up a copy of this book, the first thing you'll notice is that it is way past its freshness date, and it was that way even when Geisler quoted it back in the 1990s. Burrows' book was completed in 1957 and published the following year. The Dead Sea Scrolls were discovered in 1947, and excavations continued until 1956, one year before Burrows completed his manuscript. Solid information about the Scrolls was still a long time off, as Burrows himself states in the preface:

> "The interpretation and even the publication of the [Qumran] texts, it is true, *have only begun. No complete account will be possible for many years.* Enough progress has been made, however, to warrant a survey *of the present state* of the Dead Sea Scroll studies." (p. xi) (Emphasis added.)[22]

Burrows' survey, therefore, reflects the present state of Dead Sea Scrolls research in 1957. Anyone who is familiar with the history of the publication of the Dead Sea Scroll fragments knows that this is a very serious problem. It would take many years (read: decades) before scholars would be able to sift through all of the data, publish theories, and engage in critical peer review and debate before solid explanations and interpretations could be proposed. Burrows' book comes before any of this takes place. In fact, much of Burrows' information comes through secondhand knowledge gleaned from those who had access to the fragments at that time.

What did Burrows have to say about the Deuterocanon (Apocrypha)? Under the heading "The Apocrypha and Other Post-biblical Works; Languages and Paleography" on Page 177, Burrows discusses the different languages in which the Deuterocanon may have been originally written. He states:

---

[22] Millar Burrows, *More Light on the Dead Sea Scrolls: New Scrolls and New Interpretations* (New York: Viking Adult), 1958.

"The Qumran fragments of Sirach and Tobit have not yet been published, and not much information about them has been released. One of the Aramaic copies of Tobit is on papyrus; the other one and the Hebrew copy are on leather. The Ecclesiasticus fragments also are of leather. It may be assumed,

in the absence of information to the contrary, that all these manuscripts are non-canonical in format and script" (p. 177).

That's about it. However, even this short paragraph reveals several surprising inconsistencies with Geisler's comments.

First: Geisler repeatedly stated in his articles that the "Apocrypha" was not written on special parchment. Indeed, the footnote in the "*To Understand the Bible*" even states that they did not find any of the Deuterocanon "written on the more valuable writing materials like parchment." But Burrows, even at this early date, knew that both Tobit and Sirach were written on parchment (leather)!

Second: Burrows states that, when he wrote this chapter, the fragments of Sirach and Tobit had "not yet been published, and not much information about them has been released." This is not surprising given the date of the book, but it does explain why Burrows has so little to say about the Deuterocanon. There really wasn't any data for him to comment on. Geisler, if he was dependent on Burrows, never mentions that Burrows' findings were based on secondhand information.

Third: Burrows' conclusion that the deuterocanonical fragments were in a "non-canonical" format and script was not a statement of fact, but only an assumption. He assumed, since he didn't possess any evidence to the contrary, that the "Apocrypha" wasn't found in a special format. Geisler, however, states it as a fact.

Fourth and most surprising is that Geisler's quotation from Burrows isn't found in his comments on the "Apocrypha." If the quotation isn't taken from the Deuterocanon section, where did it come from?

Immediately after a few short comments about the deuterocanonical fragments, Burrows turns his attention to "other" manuscripts, namely the Pseudepigrapha and the sectarian writings, that were also found at Qumran. Regarding these documents, Burrows wrote:

> "The large number of *other works* represented by scrolls or fragments in the caves of the Wady Qumran is clear from the brief account of them already given (pp. 27-36). Some *of them*, we have seen, were already known in Greek or other translations and were commonly included *among the books called Pseudepigrapha. Many others* were entirely unknown until they appeared in the remains of the Qumran library. <u>There is no reason to think that any *of these works* were venerated as sacred Scripture.</u>" (p. 177-178) (Emphasis added. Geisler's quote is underlined.)

As you can see, Burrows was not commenting on the Deuterocanon, as Geisler repeatedly states, but "a large number of *other works*...commonly included among the books of the Pseudepigrapha" (emphasis added) along with *other previously unknown works*. It is in regards to *these works* that Burrows states, "There is no reason to think that any of *these books* were venerated as sacred Scripture" (emphasis added). Burrows' comments, therefore, were directed at least primarily at the Pseudepigrapha found at Qumran.

WHAT DID BURROWS SAY ABOUT THE SPECIAL PARCHMENT AND SCRIPT?

The fact that Burrows did mention a special canonical "format and script" indicates that he must have broached this subject earlier in his book. Sure enough, the format and script was discussed a few pages earlier. Speaking about what was then a current hypothesis, Burrows writes:

> "New evidence of a distinction between sacred and other literature at Qumran, which affords also a means to determine how each book was regarded, has recently been brought forward" (p. 175).

Again, this "new evidence" was "recently" brought forward back in 1957. What was this new evidence? Strangely enough, it had nothing to do with the canonicity of the Deuterocanon, but the canonicity of the book of Daniel! Burrows writes:

> "If reliable, this is important, because it indicates that one of the books in the Jewish and Hebrew canon, the book of Daniel, was not regarded as sacred Scripture in the Qumran community. The official publication of the fragments excavated in Cave 1 includes a transcription of the Daniel fragments acquired by Archbishop Samuel in 1948. Commenting on them, Barthelemy remarks

71

that in the other biblical manuscripts of Cave 1 the height of the columns is double the width, whereas the height and width of the columns in these Daniel fragments are approximately equal. Pieces of a copy of Daniel written on papyrus, Barthelemy adds, have been found in Cave 6, whereas the other biblical manuscripts in Hebrew are made of leather" (p. 175-176).

This sounds a lot like the "taller" script and special (leather) parchment mentioned in Geisler's "*To Understand the Bible...*" footnote. Did Geisler get his "special script" and "special parchment" idea from Burrows? Hopefully he didn't, since that would raise a number of issues with Geisler's presentation. For example, Burrows' "new evidence" of a biblical distinction was put forward before the publication and full disclosure of the fragments took place, so it was – even back then – entirely subject to change. Moreover, Burrows, unlike Geisler, did not present the special format idea as a fact, but rather qualified his comments with the words "If reliable." Geisler also states that the Qumran community accepted the rabbinical canon (i.e., the Protestant Old Testament canon), but if the special format idea is true (which Geisler assumes it is), then, according to Burrows, the book of Daniel was not accepted at Qumran as canonical Scripture because (at that time) there weren't any fragments found that were written in the special format.

In regards to this last point, Burrows himself notes that, even at that early date, the special script and parchment idea may not have been a reliable indicator for canonicity. In the next paragraph, Burrows references Frank M. Cross Jr., who states that subsequent discoveries had already called into question whether a strict demarcation of "canonical" texts via the use of parchment and script could be made. Burrows wrote:

> "Cross points out that since Barthelemy wrote this statement a papyrus manuscript of I-II Kings from Cave 6 has been identified. He agrees, however, that the practice of the Qumran scribes in copying biblical manuscripts was fairly uniform. They usually wrote on leather, usually made the columns twice as high as they were wide, and usually used either the old Hebrew script or the formal "bookhand" of the square script, though a very few biblical scrolls in a cursive script were found in Cave 4. Recognizing therefore that there were exceptions to the standard procedure..." (p. 176)

Where Geisler deems the special "taller" script and parchment to be definitive in regards to canonicity, Burrows states that this was not true in all cases. Citing Cross, he notes that biblical manuscripts were usually in this format, but there were exceptions. If Burrows was Geisler's source, he should have known that even Burrows found problems with the special format idea.

Now that the Dead Sea Scrolls have been published and scholars have all of the necessary information to do their work, we can find out for certain if the copyists employed a special format for biblical texts. Dead Sea Scroll expert Emmanuel Tov raises this very question in his work *Hebrew Bible, Greek Bible and Qumran: Collected Essays* (Mohr Siebeck, 2008) within a section titled "Special Procedures for Biblical Texts?" Tov writes:

"...the corpus of texts from the Judean Desert, when taken as a whole, shows that the scribes made little distinction when copying sacred and nonsacred manuscripts, and more specifically biblical and nonbiblical manuscripts. In some circles a limited or even rigid distinction was made between these two types of manuscripts... However, this distinction is not reflected in the Judean Desert texts when taken as a whole.... When reading the instruction in rabbinic literature regarding the writings of sacred texts, the impression is created that these instructions are specific to sacred texts, but from the Qumran text it is now evident that in most instances identical procedures were also applied to nonsacred texts."
(p. 126-127)

Tov continues by noting that there are some general indicators for biblical texts. For example, they are "almost exclusively" written on parchment. They were inscribed on only one side, and a deluxe format was usually used. Also, a "special stichographaic layout was devised for the writing of several poetical sections of many biblical scrolls, as well as one nonbiblical scroll."

Ironically, Tov's list of general indicators fits the deuterocanonical texts. Tobit and Sirach were both copied on parchment, and Sirach is written in a "special stichographaic" layout. In a later work, Tov writes:

"A stichographic layout is evidenced in 30 Judean Desert texts of two poems in the Torah (Exodus 15; Deuteronomy 32), Psalms (especially Psalm

119), Proverbs, Lamentations, and Job... In the Judean Desert texts, there is a special layout for poetical units that is almost exclusive to biblical texts (including Ben Sira [2QSir and MasSir]), and is not found in any of the non-biblical poetical compositions from the Judean Desert..." (*Textual Criticism of the Hebrew Bible*; Fortress Press, 2012, 201-202).

Therefore, Geisler's "tall" text and special parchment claims may have seemed plausible in 1957, but the theory was quite precarious even back then. Now that all of the data is available, we know that the scribes at Qumran didn't employ an exclusive special format for biblical texts, although there were a few general indicators. Unlike Geisler's claim, furthermore, the deuterocanonical book of Sirach was written on parchment and was found copied in a special stichographaic layout, not only at Qumran, but also at Masada.[23] It appears that the "special" biblical format actually affirms the deuterocanonical book of Sirach.

---

[23] See *Why Catholic Bibles Are Bigger*, 43 and especially "Sirach and the Judean Desert Texts" in *The Case for the Deuterocanon*, 101-106.

MISREPRESENTATION #3 JEROME FOLLOWED THE MAJORITY OPINION WHEN HE REJECTED THE DEUTEROCANON

St. Jerome (340-420) was the first early Church father to reject the Deuterocanon as Apocrypha. Articles and websites sometimes claim that Jerome's rejection reflected the majority view in the early Church. Their proof comes from a single line in St. Jerome's *Apology Against Rufinus*, where he states that he was "following the judgments of the churches" (*Apology Against Rufinus*, 33). If St. Jerome was "following the judgments of the churches," it is argued, his view must have been the majority view in antiquity.

Here is a quick summary for those who are not familiar with the history of the Church's use of the Deuterocanon. The acceptance of the Deuterocanon can be seen from the very beginning of Christianity on the pages of the New Testament. The New Testament both uses and references the Deuterocanon in a way that is indistinguishable from its use of the Old Testament.[24] With rare exceptions, the early Church fathers from the apostolic period to the time of Jerome also accepted and used the Deuterocanon as inspired Scripture capable of confirming doctrine.[25] St. Jerome was

---

[24] See *Why Catholic Bibles Are Bigger*, 30-43 and *The Case for the Deuterocanon*, 1-37.
[25] For a full summary of the evidence, please see "*The 'Canonical" Usage by the Early Christians (Consensus)*" in *The Case for the Deuterocanon*, 107-249.

the first Christian writer known to assign the Deuterocanon to the Apocrypha.[26]

Early Protestants (Luther, Calvin et al.) appealed to Jerome as proof that the early Church was undecided on the issue of the Deuterocanon or that his view represented that of antiquity. Evidence is rarely offered to support this view outside of claims that a handful of fathers excluded the Deuterocanon from their canonical lists.[27] But did St. Jerome really claim that he was "following the judgments of the churches" when he rejected the Deuterocanon as Apocrypha?

The best way to answer this question is to reproduce the context in which Jerome makes these remarks and discover whether the context supports the claim. Jerome, while commenting about what he wrote in his *Preface to the Book of Daniel*, says:

> "In reference to Daniel my answer will be that I did not say that he was not a prophet; on the contrary, I confessed in the very beginning of the Preface that he was a prophet. But I wished to show what was *the opinion upheld by the Jews*; and what were the arguments on which *they relied* for its proof. I also told the reader that the version read in the Christian churches was not that of the Septuagint translators but that of Theodotion. It is true, I said that the Septuagint version was in this book very different from the original, and that it

---

[26] See *Why Catholic Bibles are Bigger*, 85-98; *The Case for the Deuterocanon*, 275-284.

[27] This issue is treated in detail in "The Problem with Lists" in *The Case for the Deuterocanon*, 313-343.

was condemned by the right judgment of the churches of Christ; but the fault was not mine who only stated the fact, but that of those who read the version. We have four versions to choose from: those of Aquila, Symmachus, the Seventy, and Theodotion. The churches choose to read Daniel in the version of Theodotion. What sin have I committed in *following the judgment of the churches*? But when I repeat what the Jews say against the Story of Susanna and the Hymn of the Three Children, and the fables of Bel and the Dragon, which are not contained in the Hebrew Bible, the man who makes this a charge against me proves himself to be a fool and a slanderer; *for I explained not what I thought but what they commonly say against us.* I did not reply to their opinion in the Preface, because I was studying brevity, and feared that I should seem to be writing not a Preface but a book. I said therefore, 'As to which this is not the time to enter into discussion.' Otherwise from the fact that I stated that Porphyry had said many things against this prophet, and called, as witnesses of this, Methodius, Eusebius, and Apollinarius, who have replied to his folly in many thousand lines, it will be in his power to accuse me for not having written in my Preface against the books of Porphyry. If there is anyone who pays attention to silly things like this, I must tell him loudly and freely that no one is compelled to read what he does not want; that I wrote for those who asked me, not for those who would scorn me, for the grateful not the carping, for the earnest not the indifferent. Still, I wonder that a man should read the version of Theodotion the heretic and judaizer, and should scorn that of a Christian, simple and sinful though he may be." (Emphasis added.)

As you can see, Jerome's comment about "following the judgment of the churches" concerns the version of Daniel that the Church read (i.e., the Greek Theodotion version instead of the Septuagint). Although the Christian Church has always preferred the Greek Septuagint translation of the Old Testament – it is the text that the New Testament most often uses for quoting the Old Testament – such was not the case for the book of Daniel. Instead, Christians from the very beginning opted to read Daniel according to the Theodotion version, not the Septuagint. St. Jerome's comments, therefore, have nothing to do with his rejection of the Deuterocanon.

In regard to the deuterocanonical sections in Daniel (i.e., Susanna, the Hymn of the Three Children, Bel and the Dragon), Jerome addresses a misunderstanding. In his preface to Daniel, St. Jerome reproduced a few of the arguments that the rabbis launch against these deuterocanonical sections. Apparently, Rufinus, Jerome's bitter enemy, believed that Jerome reproduced these arguments because he held the same opinion. Such was not the case, as Jerome points out:

"...for I explained not what I thought but what they commonly say against us. I did not reply to their opinion in the Preface, because I was studying brevity, and feared that I should seem to be writing not a Preface but a book." (Emphasis added.)

Although St. Jerome did indeed reject the Deuterocanon (along with the deuterocanonical sections of Daniel) as Apocrypha, his rationale for doing so was very different from that of the rabbis. According to St. Jerome's view, the Hebrew text was identical to the inspired original because it was preserved only in a single version. Therefore, whatever was not found in the Hebrew text was spurious. The discovery of the Dead Sea Scrolls has shown, however, that Jerome's reasoning was incorrect.[28]

---

[28] See *Why Catholic Bibles Are Bigger*, 46-47, and the "Illicit Removal by Jerome" in *The Case for the Deuterocanon*, 275-284.

MISREPRESENTATION #4 FLORENCE'S ACCEPTANCE OF THE DEUTEROCANON BOLSTERED BELIEF IN PURGATORY.

Our next misrepresentation comes from Geisler's "Apocrypha" article in *Baker Encyclopedia of Christian Apologetics*, which asserts:

> "At the Council of Trent (1546), the infallible proclamation was made accepting the Apocrypha as part of the inspired Word of God. Some Catholic scholars claim that the earlier Council of Florence (1442) made the same pronouncement... The Council of Florence (A.D. 1442) had proclaimed the Apocrypha inspired, which helped bolster the doctrine of purgatory that had already blossomed in Roman Catholicism. However, the manifestations of this belief in the sale of indulgences came to full bloom in Luther's day, and Trent's infallible pronouncement of the Apocrypha was a clear polemic against Luther's teaching."[29]

Earlier, we encountered another reference from Geisler to Trent and its supposed "arbitrary" selection of the Deuterocanon. This section contains a number of misrepresentations.

---

[29] See Norman Geisler and Ralph MacKenzie, "*Roman Catholic and Evangelicals: Agreements and Differences*" (Grand Rapids, Baker Books), 1997, 164.

The first misrepresentation is that "some" Catholic scholars claim that the same canon was given at Florence. It's difficult to believe that any scholar, Catholic or Protestant, would deny this fact. Not only did Trent adopt the Florentine canon, but Trent even had the original decree from the Council of Florence retrieved so that it could be examined. Moreover, we have already seen earlier with the "forty-four percent" mistake that, on February 15, the fathers at Trent unanimously voted to adopt the canon as given at the Council of Florence. It's strange that this would even be questioned, since it is a matter of record.

The second misrepresentation is that Florence's reaffirmation of the Deuterocanon helped "bolster the doctrine of purgatory," as if the reaffirmation of the canon was somehow tied to the Council's words concerning purgatory. Although Second Maccabees did play an important role in Martin Luther's rejection of the Catholic understanding of purgatory, it played no such role at the Council of Florence. In fact, Florence's decree on the canon of Scripture and its treatment of purgatory were two entirely separate issues. This fact is borne out in the Acts of the Council of Florence.[30] It can also be seen in the very structure of the Florentine council. Florence was a reunion Council that sought to bring together the East and the West. To expedite matters, each of Florence's decrees was promulgated as a papal bull. In regards to the reunion with the Greek Church, the Greek Church had always accepted the inspiration and canonicity of the Deuterocanon as well as the final sanctification of the elect (i.e., purgatory). The only real difference

---

[30] *Acta Sacri Oecumenici Councilii Florentini ab Horatio instiniano: Bibliothecae Vaticanae Custde Primario; collacta, Disposita, Illustrata* (Romae, 1638), 285-286. Second Maccabees is referenced in an early discussion with the Greek theologians, but since the Greeks already believed in purgatory it served no real purpose.

concerned the nature of that purification and specifically the nature of purgatorial fire, which to the Eastern theologians at the Council seemed to be a form of *apokatastasis*.[31] Since Second Maccabees has nothing to say about this issue, the *Decree on behalf of the Greeks* (promulgated under the bull "Laetenur coeli," July 6, 1439) never mentions Second Maccabees or the Deuterocanon.

The canon was discussed in the decree on behalf of the Jacobites (bull "Cantata Domino," February 4, 1442), which concerned a very different issue. In regard to the reunion with the Jacobites of Syria, Florence stated:

> "It professes one and the same God as the author of the Old and New Testament, that is, of the Law and the Prophets and the Gospel, since the saints of both Testaments have spoken with the inspiration of the same Holy Spirit, whose books, which are contained under the following titles it accepts and venerates..."[32]

The decree then lists the protocanonical and deuterocanonical books of the Old and New Testaments, and it concludes with a condemnation of the Manicheans. As you can see, there's nothing about purgatory here. The canon and purgatory were two entirely different issues. Its reaffirmation of the canon of Scripture,

---

[31] *Apokatastasis* is the belief that the damned will eventually be saved and that the flames of Hell are to purify and restore those who are lost. This belief was condemned by the Council of Constantinople I (543) and the Second Council of Constantinople (553).

[32] *Sources of Catholic Dogma*, Henry Denzinger and Karl Rahner, eds., trans. Roy J. Deferrari (St. Louis, MO: B. Herder Book Co.), 1954, 226-227.

therefore, did nothing to "bolster" belief in purgatory, since its acceptance had long predated the Council.

For the sake of completeness, we should mention a myth that Geisler propounds at the conclusion to the paragraph quoted above. Geisler writes:

> "The official infallible addition of books that support prayers for the dead is highly suspect, coming only a few years after Luther protested this doctrine. It has all the appearance of an attempt to provide infallible support for doctrines that lack a real biblical basis."

This last statement is nothing other than a furtive fallacy, which is essentially "guilt by appearances." There is no evidence to back up these claims. In fact, what Geisler deems as "highly suspect" is actually not suspect at all. He states, for example, that Trent's adoption of the Deuterocanon is "highly suspect" because it came "only a few years after Luther protested the doctrine." When Geisler believes that Luther protested purgatory is anyone's guess. Was it October 31, 1517, when Luther nailed the Ninety-five Theses? Or was it in 1519 when Luther denied the canonicity of Second Maccabees at the Second Disputation at Leipzig? Let's assume for the sake of argument that it was in 1519. The Council of Trent convened in 1545, and it issued the decree on the canon on April 8, 1546. That means that 27 years had elapsed between the Second Leipzig Disputation and the decree on the canon. Is 27 years really "only a few years?" Is a 27-year gap really providing us with the information to pinpoint that Trent's canon was a reaction specifically directed to Luther's protest against purgatory?

Had Dr. Geisler consulted the primary sources, he would have known that the main reason that Trent chose to address the canon of Scripture and Sacred Tradition was to provide the basis upon which other doctrinal decrees would rely. It's true that decrees on the canon also dealt with the denials and doubts that Protestants had expressed about both the Old Testament Deuterocanon and the New Testament Deuterocanon. Geisler's claim that Trent's canon was a reaction specifically to Luther's denial of purgatory, however, is nothing more than a myth.

MISREPRESENTATION #5 THE NEW CATHOLIC ENCYCLOPEDIA SAYS TRENT IS THE FIRST INFALLIBLE DECREE ON THE CANON

Whenever you find the same quotation scattered around the Internet and edited in exactly the same way, you know that the article has been copied. This next misrepresentation came to my attention when numerous sites claimed that the *New Catholic Encyclopedia* taught that the canon of Scripture wasn't settled until the Council of Trent in the 1500s. What stood out is that they all gave the same lengthy quotation, with the ellipses in the exact same places. Either all of these sites just so happened to exclude the exact same material, or they were copied and pasted from a single source. Another oddity was the unconventional endnote that followed the quotation. Instead of giving a single reference for the quote, the endnote gives four citations. For example, one website includes the following endnote:

> "....New Catholic Encyclopedia, Vol. II, Bible, III (Canon), p. 390; Canon, Biblical, p. 29; Bible, III (Canon), p. 390, as quoted in Webster, The Old Testament Canon and the Apocrypha, 50-51."[33]

Thankfully, this website was kind enough to acknowledge that the quote came from a secondary source, namely William Webster's

---

[33] As quoted in Aaron Brake's "Is the Apocrypha Scripture?" http://pleaseconvinceme.com/2012/is-the-apocrypha-scripture.

"The Old Testament Canon and the Apocrypha." Here is the quote as given in Webster:

> "In fact, the New Catholic Encyclopedia states that the canon was not officially settled for the Western Church as a whole until the Council of Trent in the sixteenth century:
>
> 'St. Jerome distinguished between canonical books and ecclesiastical books. The latter he judged were circulated by the Church as good spiritual reading but were not recognized as authoritative Scripture. The situation remained unclear in the ensuing centuries...for example, John of Damascus, Gregory the Great, Walafrid, Nicholas of Lyra and Tostado continued to doubt the canonicity of the deuterocanonical books... According to Catholic doctrine, the proximate criterion of the biblical canon is the infallible decision of the Church. This decision was not given until rather late in the history of the Church at the Council of Trent... The Council of Trent definitively settled the matter of the Old Testament Canon. That this had not been done previously is apparent from the uncertainty that persisted up to the time of Trent.'"[34]

Webster later concludes:

---

[34] William Webster, *The Old Testament Canon and the Apocrypha* (Battle Ground, WA: Christian Resources, Inc.), 2002, 50-51.

"The New Catholic Encyclopedia states that the
reason the canon was not definitively settled for
the Church until the Council of Trent is that the
issue remained unclear in the centuries
subsequently to Jerome; meaning that many
leading theologians, cardinals, and bishops did not
accept the Apocrypha as canonical."[35]

Although Webster seems to be quoting the New Catholic
Encyclopedia, did the Encyclopedia really say what Webster claims
it says? Also, why did this single quotation require three citations?
A quick trip to the local library was in order.

Upon finding the encyclopedia, I quickly flipped open to the entry
titled "Biblical Canon." The article is composed of three parts that
are written by three different authors. Fr. William Most penned the
introduction (p. 20-22), while the "History of the Old Testament
Canon," which is partially quoted by Webster, was written by J. C.
Turro (p. 22-27). The final section on the "History of the New
Testament Canon" (p. 27-34) was written by R. E. Murphy.

Webster's quotation is found in a subsection in Turro's section
titled "Canon of the Old Testament Among Christians." Webster's
quote gives the impression that the article states that there was no
real agreement on the Deuterocanon prior to the Council of Trent.
But is this what the article really says?

A glance at J. C. Turro's article reveals that his focus is on Christian
usage and not the dogmatic pronouncements of the Church. He
never mentions Pope Damasus I (the council of Rome), the
councils of Hippo Regius, Carthage III, and Carthage IV, or

---

[35] *ibid.* 51.

statements by Pope St. Innocent I, Pope Gelasius I, Pope Hormisdas, or Pope Nicholas I. The Ecumenical Council of Florence is mentioned, but only to show that both the East and the West accepted the Deuterocanon and that Florence used the deuterocanonical books in its decrees. This focus on usage rather than dogmatic pronouncement can be seen in Turro's own outline for the section:

> "In the history of the OT canon among Christians, note should be taken of the use of the OT in the NT, of the attitude of the Fathers and writings in the Western Church until the Council of Trent, of the canon in the Eastern Churches, and of the divergences between the Catholic and the Protestant canons of the OT." (p. 26)

The Council of Trent is mentioned only to supply an endpoint for his survey of the writings of the fathers in the West. This point, as we will see, will be important later on.

The article makes a number of points leading up to Webster's quote. It states, "An examination of the NT use of the OT shows that the NT writers had the same broad view of the sacred books as the Hellenist and Qumran Jews had of them." In other words, the New Testament writers "knew and used a fuller collection that included the so-called deuterocanonical books." It continues by noting the early Church's use of the Greek Septuagint, which intermixed the Deuterocanon with the protocanonical books. Hence, the form of the Septuagint contributed to the "...acceptance of these books as an integral part of the OT" in the early Church.

Under the title "Canon of the Western Church" (from which Webster draws part of his quote), the text states quite frankly "the consensus of the Church through the 2nd and 3rd centuries was favorable to the full OT catalogue." When did Christians begin to have doubts about the Deuterocanon, then? Turro suggests that the rejection in rabbinical Judaism led some Christians to have "hesitations" and that these hesitations "gradually evolved into misgivings" about the Deuterocanon's canonicity.

Turro then makes a very important point: "Attitudes towards the canon through the next several centuries were marked by a curious discrepancy between statement and practice. Several writers express themselves in favor of the restricted Hebrew canon; yet, in practice, they freely employ the deuterocanonical books as Scripture." My own research into this issue, which is explained in detail in *Why Catholic Bibles Are Bigger*, confirms Turro's observation. Scholars in the Middle Ages often gave the ancient equivalent of a "hat tip" or a "shout out" to St. Jerome by quoting his prefaces, but many of these scholars (who are often listed as those who rejected the Deuterocanon) used the Deuterocanon as inspired Scripture capable of confirming doctrine. These authors, as Turro says, "... seem to imply that the deuterocanonical works were of lesser authority than the protocanonical books, [but] they nonetheless admit that they were received by the Church, and thus they implicitly attest to their authoritative status."

Turro then turns his attention to St. Jerome (a section which is partially quoted by Webster). He begins by stating exactly what Webster quotes: St. Jerome distinguished between "canonical books" and "ecclesiastical books." The latter, he judged, were circulated by the Church as good "spiritual reading."

As Webster's quote then adds an ellipsis, we must ask what Turro wrote after mentioning St. Jerome. Turro states that St. Augustine (354-430) accepted the Septuagint (LXX) and the Deuterocanon, which St. Jerome rejected as apocrypha. He also notes that St. Augustine's view prevailed (apparently over St. Jerome's opinion) and that the Deuterocanon remained in the Latin Vulgate. Webster omits all of this information.

This is a long summary, so let's quickly recap some of Turro's main points: (1) the New Testament was held to be a "fuller collection" of books that included the Deuterocanon; (2) the "consensus of the Church through the 2nd and 3rd centuries was favorable" to the Deuterocanon; (3) doubts developed in the East in the 4th century; (4) at the end of the 4th/beginning of the 5th century, St. Jerome rejected the Deuterocanon as apocrypha; (5) Augustine accepted the fuller canon and his favorable view "prevailed"; (6) the attitude of scholars "through the next several centuries were marked by a curious discrepancy" of quoting Jerome while using the Deuterocanon as inspired Scripture; (7) although some of these scholars imply that the Deuterocanon is "lesser" than the Protocanon, their use nevertheless shows that the Deuterocanon was accepted in the Church.

Now that we have the larger context in mind, let's turn our attention to Webster's quotation, which reads:

> "The situation remained unclear in the ensuing centuries...for example, John of Damascus, Gregory the Great, Walafrid, Nicholas of Lyra and Tostado continued to doubt the canonicity of the deuterocanonical books... According to Catholic doctrine, the proximate criterion of the biblical

canon is the infallible decision of the Church. This decision was not given until rather late in the history of the Church at the Council of Trent... The Council of Trent definitively settled the matter of the Old Testament Canon. That this had not been done previously is apparent from the uncertainty that persisted up to the time of Trent."

Here is what Turro's article in the *New Catholic Encyclopedia* actually says:

"The situation remained unclear in the ensuing centuries, although the tendency to accept the disputed books was becoming all the time more general. In spite of this trend some, e.g., John Damascene, Gregory the Great, Walafrid, Nicholas of Lyra and Tostado continued to doubt the canonicity of the deuterocanonical books. St. THOMAS AQUINAS has for a long time been listed as a dissenter because of his supposed doubts about Wisdom and Sirach, but P. Synave has argued convincingly to clear him of this imputation [*Revue biblique* 21 (1924) 522-533]. The Council of Trent definitively settled the matter of the OT Canon. That this had not been done previously is apparent from the uncertainty that persisted up to the time of Trent." (Emphasis theirs.)

As you can see, Webster's ellipses change the meaning of Turro's paragraph. Webster begins by omitting Turro's statement that from the time of Jerome (5th century) to Trent (1545), "the tendency to accept the disputed books [i.e., the Deuterocanon] was becoming all the time more general." Whatever doubts Jerome aroused among Christian writers, the tendency to accept the Deuterocanon became more general. By omitting this clause, Webster gives his readers the impression that the situation had remained unchanged since Jerome's rejection. Turro says that the trend was swinging against Jerome and in favor of the Deuterocanon.

Even worse, Webster then omits the beginning clause of the next sentence. Instead of reproducing Turro, who states:

> "The situation remained unclear in the ensuing centuries, although the tendency to accept the disputed books was becoming all the time more general. In spite of this trend some, e.g., John Damascene, Gregory the Great, Walafrid, Nicholas of Lyra and Tostado continued to doubt..."

Webster reframes it to read:

> "The situation remained unclear in the ensuing centuries...for example, John of Damascus, Gregory the Great, Walafrid, Nicholas of Lyra and Tostado continued to doubt... "

Notice that Webster has deliberately omitted all of Turro's comments about the existence of a trend. By continuing the quote after excluding the beginning clause, Webster makes it appear that Turro is providing typical examples of those who doubted, when in fact these names are given as examples of those who still doubted despite the ever-growing trend of acceptance. These individuals were outliers among the growing acceptance, not representatives from the mainstream, as Webster's quote implies. Webster also changes the original text of Turro by striking the abbreviation "e.g." (*exempli gratia*) and replacing it with the English translation "for example." Had the text been left as it was originally published, it would read:

> "The situation remained unclear in the ensuing centuries...e.g., John Damascene, Gregory the Great, Walafrid, Nicholas of Lyra and Tostado continued to doubt..."

The sheer awkwardness of this phrasing would flag the reader that Webster had cut out something important, so the abbreviation was translated so as to read more smoothly, as if the ellipsis simply skipped over irrelevant material.

Webster rightly cut out the comments about St. Thomas, but you may have noticed that something is missing. In the original Turro article, where does he say, "According to Catholic doctrine, the proximate criterion of the biblical canon is the infallible decision of the Church. This decision was not given until rather late in the history of the Church at the Council of Trent..."? This statement is not found in the original paragraph. In fact, it's not found anywhere in Turro's article. Here is where Webster's odd endnote comes in.

The statement doesn't come from Turro. The second citation given in the endnote directs the reader to the *New Catholic Encyclopedia* article, "Canon, biblical, p. 29." If you flip to page 29, however, you'll notice that there is no such article. Thinking that it was a typo and that it meant to read page 290, I flipped over to page 290 and found nothing. After some digging, I found the passage. It wasn't in volume two of the *New Catholic Encyclopedia* where Turro's article resides, but in volume three! The endnote, oddly enough, fails to inform the reader that Webster has inserted a quote from a similar article within a different volume written by a different author!

The two sentences inserted into Turro come from a very brief two hundred and thirty two word summary on the canon of Scripture written by L. F. Hartman. Here is the relevant material from this passage:

> "CANON, BIBLICAL, the official list of the inspired books that constitute Sacred Scripture. Since divine inspiration pertains to the realm of the supernatural, the fact of inspiration can be known only through divine revelation. According to Catholic doctrine, the proximate criterion of the Biblical canon is the infallible decision of the Church. This decision was not given until rather late in the history of the Church (at the Council of Trent). Before that time there was some doubt about the canonicity of certain Biblical books, i.e., about their belonging to the canon... For a fuller treatment of the Biblical canon and its history, see BIBLE, III (CANON)."

Short summaries almost always lack a certain amount of precision, which is probably why Hartman directs his readers to "a fuller treatment" in Turro's article. Unfortunately, Hartman's brevity certainly comes at the expense of precision, since what he says about Trent needs a little bit more qualification. If you compare the Old Testament canon article of the original 1908 *Catholic Encyclopedia* with Hartman's comments, you'll see what I mean. The 1908 article states:

> "The Tridentine decrees from which the above list is extracted was the first infallible *and effectually* promulgated pronouncement on the Canon, addressed to the Church Universal." (*Catholic Encyclopedia*, "Canon of the Old Testament") (Emphasis added.)

Notice the double qualification. Trent was the "first infallible *and effectually* promulgated pronouncement " Previous councils and papal decrees had infallibly settled the issue of the canon centuries before Trent, but it didn't bring about universal conformity in practice. Hartman seems to allude to this by noting that, "Before that time [i.e., the Council of Trent] there was doubt about the canonicity of certain Bible books..." The implication is that uniformity was achieved after Trent; that is to say, Trent effactually settled the matter. By omitting Hartman's statement concerning some doubting and transplanting Hartman's words into Turro's article, the impression is given that Turro is stating that there was no infallible definition of the canon prior to Trent, which is not true.

This is nothing new for Church councils, even Ecumenical Councils. The Councils may settle the matter in terms of doctrine, but this doesn't stop dissenters and heretics from laboring against it. Take, for example, the great Council of Nicaea (325). It definitively, authoritatively, and infallibly defined that the Son is consubstantial with the Father. However, Arianism persisted. The point is that, even if a Council doesn't effectually close an issue since some errors may persist for years or maybe even centuries afterward, the matter is nevertheless doctrinally settled. The same is true with the canon of Scripture. As both of my books show, the canon was defined back in the fourth century, but because Jerome's erroneous views about the Deuterocanon continued to circulate in the prefaces of the Latin Bible (called the Vulgate), some individuals in the West uncritically followed the great saint's opinion.

As the Catholic biblical scholar Francis Gigot observed:

> "If now we inquire into the causes of this persistent division between the ecclesiastical writings of the Middle Ages, we shall find that its main, *if not its exclusive cause*, is the influence which the views of St. Jerome exercised upon the minds of many Doctors of that period... It is not therefore to be wondered at, if the view so unfavorable to the deuterocanonical books, which these prefaces contained, seemed tenable to many schoolmen, and were, in fact, held by them in the teeth of contrary practice in the Church, and of disciplinary decrees of the Popes." (Gigot, *General Introduction to the Study of Sacred Scripture*, 68-69) (Emphasis added.)

The various scholars from the Middle Ages that Webster chronicles in his books attest to the truth of Gigot's statement.

A careful reader may have noticed that Webster's jump back to Turro is awkward. The splicing produced a redundancy in the Webster quote, since the Hartman quote ends with the words "the

Council of Trent" and Turro's new line begins with the same words, making it read, "the history of the Church at the Council of Trent...The Council of Trent definitively settled..." Unless the reader was able to decipher the citations in the endnote and look up the texts, this strange redundancy is the only clue for the reader that the quotation has now returned back to the original author and article.

The final quote from Turro is:

> "The Council of Trent definitively settled the matter of the OT Canon. That this had not been done previously is apparent from the uncertainty that persisted up to the time of Trent."

What does Turro mean by "the matter?" What was the matter? Here is where Webster's insertion of Hartman's comments misrepresents Turro's article. What was the matter of the OT canon that needed to be addressed? If all that you read was Webster's quote, it would appear that "the matter" was the lack of a "proximate criterion of the biblical canon" that needed to be satisfied by an "infallible decision of the Church." Trent infallibly settled the matter for the first time. Therefore, the Old Testament canon was something of an open question before Trent. This reading is possible only because Webster has changed the preceding context. Turro didn't say that *an infallible decree* was needed, as if one had never been given prior to Trent, but rather that *uniformity in practice* hadn't been achieved. Trent was the first infallible *and effectual* decree on the canon. Whatever dissent existed prior to the Council on the canon no longer persisted within the Church.

INDEX

Akiva ben Joseph, 22

Alexandrian canon, 17

Amos, 41, 42

anathema, 51, 52, 53

Apocalypse of Esdras, 23, 24, 26, 27

Apocryphon of Joshua, 65

apokatastasis, 85

Apollinarius, 79

Apology Against Rufinus, 77

Aquila translation, The, 79

Aquinas, St. Thomas, 95

Arabic, 32

Aramaic, 15, 16, 18, 30, 32, 66, 69

Arianism, 99

Assumption of Moses, The, 60

Augustine, St., 25, 93, 94

Baker Encyclopedia of Christian Apologetics, 47, 59, 65, 83

Barthelemy, Dominique, 72, 73

Baruch, 8, 16, 59

Book of Enoch, The, 60

Burrows, Millar, 66, 67, 68, 69, 70, 71, 72, 73

Calvin, John, 78

Calvinists, 48

canon of Scripture, The, 8

Cantata Domino, (February 4, 1442), 85

Carthage III, The council of, 24, 91

Carthage IV, The council of, 24, 91

Catholic Encyclopedia, The, 33, 98

City of God, The, 25

Clement V, Pope, 30, 32

Code of Canon Law, The, 32, 52

Concilium Tridentinum, 51, 52

Constantinople, Synod of, 47, 48, 85

"Council of Jamnia" myth, The, 21

Cross Jr., Frank M., 73

Daniel, 7, 8, 39, 44, 66, 71, 72, 78, 80, 81

De Canonicis Scripturis, 51

De Soto, Domingo, 30

Dead Sea Scrolls, The, 45, 63, 66, 67, 68, 73, 81

Decree on behalf of the Greeks, 85

Deuteronomy, 41, 42, 44, 75

Dublin Review, The, 30, 31, 32

Ecclesiastes, 21, 39, 44

Esther, 7, 8, 39, 44

Eusebius, 79

excommunication, 52

Exodus, 31, 41, 42, 44, 75

103

Ezekiel, 39, 44

Ezra, 16, 39

Final Judgment, The, 25, 26

First Chronicles, 39

First Corinthians, 41, 42

First Kings, 41

First Maccabees, 16

First Peter, 41

First Timothy, 41

Florence, The council of, 24, 52, 53, 83, 84, 85, 91

Foreiro, Francisco, 31

Galatians, 41

Geisler, Norman, 23, 47, 48, 59, 60, 61, 63, 64, 65, 67, 69, 70, 72, 73, 75, 83, 86, 87

Gelasius, Pope, 24, 91

Genesis, 16, 31, 41, 44

Gigot, Francis, 100

Gospel of Mary, The, 60

Greek, 15, 16, 18, 29, 30, 31, 32

Greek Orthodox, 48, 49

Gregory the Great, Pope St., 25, 26, 90, 94, 95, 96, 97

Habakkuk, 45

Hartman, L. F., 98, 99, 101

Hebrew, 15, 16, 22, 29, 30, 31, 32, 66

Hebrew Bible, Greek Bible and Qumran, 73

Hebrew only Myth, 15

Hebrews, The Epistle to the, 40

Hippo Regius, The council of, 24, 91

Holden, Joseph, 66

Innocent I, Pope St., 24, 91

Inspiration, 9

Isaiah, 31, 41, 42, 45

Jaffa, The synod of, 47, 48

James, The Epistle of, 41, 42

Jamnia, the council of, 22

Jeremiah, 16, 41, 42

Jerome, St., 77, 78, 80, 81, 90, 91, 93, 94, 99, 100

Jerusalem, The synod of, 47

Job, 31, 41, 65, 75

John Fisher, St., 32

John of Damascus, 90, 94, 96

John XXII, Pope, 32

John, The Gospel According to, 41

Jonah, The book of, 40

Jubilees, The book of, 66

Judith, 8, 16, 59

Laetenur coeli, (July 6, 1439), 85

Lamentations, 39, 44, 75

Larger Catechism (1839), The, 47, 48, 49

Latin, 29, 32, 94, 100

Leviticus, 41

Lewis, Jack P., 21

Lippomani, Aloysii, 30, 31

Lucaris, Cyril Patriarch, 48

Luke, The Gospel According to, 40

Luther, Martin, 78, 84

Malachi, 41

Mansoor, Menahem, 66

Mark, The Gospel According
   to, 41, 42

Masada, 75

Masoretic text, 18, 22

Matthew, The Gospel
   According to, 40

Methodius, 79

Metzger, Bruce M., 51, 52,
   53

Micah, 41, 46

*More Light on the Dead Sea
   Scrolls*, 67

Most, William, 91

Murphy, R. E., 91

Nahum, 46

New American Bible, The,
   59

*New Catholic Encyclopedia,
   The*, 89, 90, 91, 95, 97

Nicaea (325), The Council
   of, 99

Nicholas of Lyra, 90, 94, 95,
   96, 97

Ninety-five Theses, 86

Oleaster, Jerome, 30, 31

Orthodox Church, 47, 48

Ott, Ludwig, 25

paleo-Hebrew, 64, 65

Palestinian canon, 17

papyrus, 64, 69, 72, 73

parchment, 63, 64, 65, 66,
   67, 69, 72, 73, 74, 75

Pentateuch, 31, 44, 64, 65

pesher, 45, 46

Philo of Alexandria, 43, 45

*Popular Handbook of
   Archaeology and the Bible*,
   66

Porphyry, 79

Preface to the Book of Daniel,
   78

Proverbs, 75

Psalms, 41

Pseudepigrapha, The, 66, 70,
   71

purgatory, 23, 24, 25, 27,
   83, 84, 85, 86, 87

Qumran, 45, 46, 63, 64, 65,
   66, 68, 69, 70, 71, 72, 73,
   74, 75, 92

Rabbinical Judaism, 19

Reuss, Eduard, 31

Revelation, The book of, 42

Romans, 3, 41, 42

Rufinus, 80

Russian Orthodox, 48

Ruth, 39, 44

Salmeron, Alphonsus, 30, 31

Salmon, George, 29, 30, 31,
   32, 33

Second Chronicles, 39

Second Disputation at
   Leipzig, 86

Second Maccabees, 8, 16, 23,
   24, 26, 27, 84, 85, 86

Second Samuel, 41, 42

sententia communis, 25

Septuagint, 18, 22, 78, 80,
   92, 93

Septuagint, The, 18

Sirach, 8, 16, 59, 63, 64, 69, 74, 75, 95
Song of Songs, 21, 39, 44
Sources of Catholic Dogma, 85
Spinoza, Baruch, 21
St. John's College, 32
stichographaic layout, 74, 75
Sundberg, A. C., 18
Symmachus, 79
Synave, P., 95
The New Testament Canon: It's Origin, Development, and Significance, 51
Theodotion version, 78, 79, 80
To Understand the Bible Look for Jesus: The Bible Student's Guide to the Bible's Central Theme, 66, 69
Tobit, 8, 16, 59, 63, 64, 66, 69, 74
Tostado, 90, 94, 95, 96, 97
Tov, Emmanuel, 73, 74
Trent, The Council of, 13, 23, 24, 27, 29, 31, 32, 33, 51, 52, 53, 83, 84, 86, 87, 89, 90, 91, 92, 94, 95, 97, 98, 99, 100, 101
Turro, J. C., 91, 92, 93, 94, 95, 96, 97, 98, 99, 100, 101
Two-canon myth, The, 17, 18, 19
Vienne, The council of, 32
Walafrid, 90, 94, 95, 96, 97

Webster, William, 89, 90, 91, 92, 93, 94, 95, 96, 97, 100, 101
Westcott, J. B., 29, 30, 33
Wisdom, The book of, 59, 95
Zechariah, 41

Made in the USA
Las Vegas, NV
17 January 2022

41708214R00065